WALKING WITH
THE RISEN CHRIST

A Primer For Healthy
Small Groups

WALKING WITH THE RISEN CHRIST

A Primer For Healthy Small Groups

SOO-INN TAN

Walking with the Risen Christ

Copyright © 2017 Soo-Inn Tan

Published by Graceworks Private Limited
22 Sin Ming Lane
#04-76 Midview City
Singapore 573969
Tel: 67523403
Email: enquiries@graceworks.com.sg
Website: www.graceworks.com.sg

All Scripture quotations, unless otherwise noted, are taken from the *Holy Bible*, New International Version®. NIV®. Copyright © 1973, 1978, 1984, 2011 by International Bible Society. Used by permission of Zondervan. All rights reserved.

A CIP record for this book is available from the National Library Board, Singapore

Design by Intent Design and Consultancy Pte Ltd

ISBN: 978-981-11-2814-1

Printed in Singapore

2 3 4 5 6 7 8 9 10 • 25 24 23 22 21 20 19 18 17

Contents

Foreword

A fundamental discovery in the Christian life is that learning Jesus' way of life depends upon him — that is, upon his *person*. Knowing and serving God always implies *relationship with Jesus*. We must involve ourselves with the one who says, "I am the way, the truth, and the life. No one comes to the Father except through me" (John 14:6).

Sadly we Christians in the 21st century live in constant search of the next technique or tip or program for how to get ahead in the Christian life. But the Christian life is not a methodology, it is Jesus himself. As I read Soo-Inn's words here on small groups I was reminded of this critical distinction.

Certainly much has been said and written about small groups over the years, but what Soo-Inn guides us into here is what has not been said and practiced enough in the life of our small group ministries — that is, the risen Christ among us as we gather together. Jesus by his Spirit sits across the table or on the other side of the living room or class room as the central member of our small group.

By inviting us as readers to place ourselves into the story of those two disciples heading toward Emmaus (Luke 24:13–35), Soo-Inn wisely draws the mindset and practice of our small group ministries into the profound mystery of Christian community — that is, the life of God in Christ among us in the Spirit. Jesus is far more involved in things than we have any idea. He startles us with his wisdom and creativity and presence amidst the most unlikely of situations and relationships.

I have sat in many, many small groups over the years, sometimes as a member, sometimes as the leader for the group. Over and again a great temptation is to proceed in our reflecting and discussing, and even praying together, as if we were, as James Houston puts it, "talking about God behind his back." It is a wonderful moment when God by his Spirit "taps us on the shoulder" and we realize he has been there among us all along. Our groups take on so much more of an honest, lively, and transformative character when we discover together the risen Christ among us. In addition to many helpful practicalities for leading a small group, much of what you will find in these pages will help you remain alert to God's gentle and humble "tapping on your shoulder" as you lead a group.

May we all increasingly come to envision ourselves as those fellow disciples on their way to Emmaus on that first resurrection Sunday, helping one another sort out the nitty-gritty stuff of our lives, always alert and expectant to the risen Jesus coming near us and walking with us. Blessings to you and your fellow companions as you read.

Robert Loane
VantagePoint3 Ministries
Sioux Falls, South Dakota
December 2, 2016

Introduction

Most churches today have some form of small-group ministry. This is a result of two things: First, the realisation that the Christian faith is meant to be a communal faith. Second, that the main gathering of most churches, the Sunday morning worship, does not allow for the one-another, face-to-face connecting essential for community.

For the first 300 years of the church, God's people met in homes. The earliest churches were house churches of about 30–50 people meeting in homes. Official church buildings only came after the conversion of Constantine and the adoption of Christianity as the official religion of the Roman Empire

House churches were especially suited for the high degree of community that were meant to characterise the church. Some churches today have tried to go back to the house church as the basic expression of church life to varying degrees of success. I think more churches should seriously think about how they can do house churches in the 21st century.

But there are parts of the world where doing house churches will be very difficult. And many churches will be doing community in small groups. Therefore we need to continue to revisit how we do small-group ministry and how we can do better.

Often the approach to small groups is functional. It is seen as a structure that serves a key function — community. Therefore the focus is on how small groups can function well or better. I think this results in the small groups missing out on the most critical relationship — their relationship with the risen Christ.

The most important factor that dictates whether a Christian small group does what it is supposed to do — provide a context for her members to love one another — is the understanding that the group members relate to each other through their common relationship with the risen Christ.

One immediate implication of this is that groups must understand that all that happens in the meeting takes place in the presence of the risen Christ. And while it is important to structure small-group meetings — many function with the 4 Ws, Welcome, Worship, Word and Works — it is more important to understand how all these practices and any others are related to the fact that the risen Christ is in the midst of the group meeting.

Relating to God is basic and foundational to anything we do missionally, but for some reason, we don't often talk about this. When I read most books on small groups, little is said about God's presence. They contain a lot of tactical information and practical skill training. I read articles on group leadership and it is easy to find information on how to ask good questions, ideas for creative study materials, and instructions on what leaders do in order to be effective. I would rather be part of a group that gets all of the tactical stuff wrong but yet encounters Jesus on a regular basis, than miss out on the presence of God while getting the technical steps to group leadership right.

M. Scott Boren, *Missional Small Groups* (Grand Rapids, MI: BakerBooks, 2010), 70.

This short book will look at seven marks of a small group that takes seriously the fact that the risen Christ is in their midst. It does not propose a new programme. The seven marks can be adapted and applied to small groups that run different small-group programmes. The marks are derived from Luke 24:13–35, the account of the encounter of two disciples with the risen Christ on the road to Emmaus. It is hoped that this book will help revive the life of small groups as they too encounter the risen Christ in their meetings.

1

The risen Christ is the **focus** of our group meetings

REFLECTION

"As they talked and discussed these things with each other, Jesus himself came up and walked along with them;"
(LUKE 24:15)

The first mark of a healthy small group is that the group recognises the real presence of Christ in their midst as they meet. Followers of Jesus are called to follow Him in the presence of friends (John 9–17). A small group may be aware of the things they need to do: singing, study of Bible, etc., and the members may enjoy each other's company, but they may forget that Christ is among them.

Wadell's understanding of spiritual friendship helps us understand the purpose of small groups and the need to be Christ-aware:

> ... spiritual friendship is a discipleship life, a way in which people who are committed to growing in Christ help one another imitate Christ and grow in gospel virtues. Spiritual friends, through their life together, learn from one another what discipleship means and how we can acquire and develop the attitudes and virtues of Christ — they help each other

become better friends of God. (*Becoming Friends*, 108)

A healthy small group is one where the members help each other "become friends of God" and a key way that happens is being aware that Christ, their divine friend, is really among them as they meet.

What are some of the things you would do if you were to encounter Christ personally?

1. Worship Him.
2. Confess your sins to Him and ask for His forgiveness.
3. Thank Him for His blessings.
4. Ask Him for help for yourself and/or for others.
5. Ask Him for answers and guidance on matters you are facing.

Well, Christ is there in your group meeting in the person of the Holy Spirit.

The Emmaus road incident also tells us that sometimes the presence of Christ is not accessible to our senses (...they were kept from recognizing him, v.16). But whether we feel His presence or not, Christ walks among us. In the words of the old Orthodox greeting:

Declaration: "Christ is in our midst."

Response: "He is and ever shall be."

This then is the first and most important mark of a healthy small group. Their meetings are Christ-aware and Christ-directed.

READING

"We have repeatedly seen, from Aristotle on, that all friendship is based on *koinonia,* a 'third factor' held in common by the friends. In the case at hand, this third factor is not a particular interest or object but the Risen Christ, made present in the community by the activity of the Holy Spirit. 'Where two or three are gathered together in my Name, I am there in their midst,' said Jesus (Matthew 18:20). To put it succinctly, Christian friendship is friendship *in Christ.* It must endeavor by all means possible to keep the living Christ as its focus. This means rooting itself in prayer, in reflection on the word of God, in the celebration of the sacraments — all realities that point beyond the human dimension of the community to what gives it its identity and cohesion."

Brother John of Taize, *Friends In Christ* (Maryknoll, NY: Orbis Books, 2012), 134.

Recommendations

1 The opening prayer should be addressed to God and include a request for the Lord to help the group to be aware of His presence.

2 Worship with singing should be directed to the Lord and not treated as just a warm up to other things like the Bible study.

3 All components of the meeting should be done with openness to what the risen Christ is saying to us.

2
The risen Christ **speaks** to us through the Word

REFLECTION

"And beginning with Moses and all the Prophets, he explained to them what was said in all the Scriptures concerning himself."
(LUKE 24:27)

How does the living Christ speak to us? Mainly through the Bible.

Many small groups study the Bible as part of their programme. Indeed some groups are basically Bible studies and the study of the Word is the highlight of their meetings. The trouble is many groups study the Bible for its content alone. Their goal is comprehension, to answer correctly questions that help guide one to understood a given passage. But mastering biblical content may not necessarily lead to an encounter with the living Christ.

We do need to understand the Bible correctly. When Jesus appeared to a bigger group of disciples later in Chapter 24, we are told that "...he opened their minds so they could understand the Scriptures." (v.45) There are rules of Bible interpretation that help us to understand the intended meaning of the Bible. We do need to interpret the Bible accurately.

But the disciples who met Jesus on the Emmaus

road observed, "Were not our hearts burning within us while he talked with us on the road and opened the Scriptures to us?" (v.32) It is not enough to understand the Bible accurately. We need to study the Bible personally as well. We need to encounter Jesus, the Living Word, through the written Word. I suspect that the two disciples were initially prevented from recognising the person of Christ in order to prepare them for the time when Christ would return to the Father. The main place to meet Christ then would be in the Scriptures — where the Spirit of Christ would speak to them, and to us, through the Word. A key question in our study of the Scriptures then is, "What is the Lord saying to us in the passage we are studying?"

Paul reminds us that, "All Scripture is God-breathed and is useful for teaching, rebuking, correcting and training in righteousness...." (2 Timothy 3:16) Therefore our goal in Bible study is to hear from the Lord so that our thinking and behaviour is transformed by our encounter. Our goal in Bible study then is not just information. It is to seek a life-changing encounter with the Lord.

This then is the second mark of a healthy small group. They listen to the risen Christ through studying the Bible with heart and mind.

READING

'Jesus says that of all the genres of all the books in the library, the Bible most closely resembles a personal memoir. It is God's self-revelation; it's literally a book authored by God that unveils his heart, mind, and Spirit. Someone once said, 'We come to Scripture not to learn a subject but to steep ourselves in a Person.'

A right understanding of Scripture makes all the difference in the world for hearing God. It means we meditate on Scripture to hear his voice. It is in meeting him there, in his self-revealed word, that we will hear him. Yes, of course we'll also change how we behave. But we change because we've seen God; we change because he himself has spoke to us.'

Samuel C. Williamson, *Hearing God in Conversation* (Grand Rapids, MI: Kregel Publications, 2016), 57.

RECOMMENDATIONS

1   A study guide and/or study Bible can help us to understand a passage accurately. We must guard against people making the text say what they want.

2   If you use a study guide, do not feel obliged to answer every question in a given chapter. The Bible study leader can select what are the key questions that need to be addressed in a given meeting. The idea is to give adequate time for understanding, listening, and application. The study guide is a tool, not the master.

3   The study should conclude by asking how we need to live in response to what the Lord has said to us through the study. When appropriate, specific plans can be shared with the group, providing accountability and encouragement for members to respond appropriately to what they have heard.

3

The risen Christ encourages us to **be honest** with Him and with each other

REFLECTION

"They stood still, their faces downcast."
(LUKE 24:17b)

A small group is defined by two key relationships. First, is their relationship with the risen Christ. Second, is the relationship between the members of the group. Healthy relationships are based on honest sharing. We note that the two disciples on the Emmaus road did not hide their true feelings from each other. Their hopes had been crushed because they believed Jesus had been executed. Their faces showed their discouragement. They did not hide their true feelings.

Gareth Weldon Icenogle, adapting the work of John Powell, suggests that there are five levels of face-to-face communication.

Level One: Cliché Communication. This represents the least willingness to share ourselves. In fact there is no intentional communication here at all, but conversation that avoids engagement.

Level Two: Reporting the Facts. This represents a minimal sharing of ourselves — a sharing of objective knowledge. Raw knowledge is communicated without personal reflection.

Level Three: Sharing my Ideas and Opinions. This represents giving more of my individual and unique self. I am the only one with these specific ideas or opinions.

Level Four: Sharing my Feelings, Values or Emotions. These words represent my more personal self. I am now speaking out of a more hidden part of my being.

Level Five: Confessional sharing. This represents peak communication. These are the experiences and feelings I may not ever share with another.

(*Biblical Foundations For Small Group Ministry* [Downers Grove, IL: InterVarsity Press, 1994], 76–77.)

Normal human communication would include all five levels. But healthy small groups are places where one can communicate at the deepest levels if need be, places where we can share our deepest pains and our highest joys.

The presence of Christ in our meetings makes it a safe place for us to share our lives. As we open our hearts to the Lord, we open our hearts to each other.

This then is the third mark of a healthy small group. In an increasingly lonely world, it provides a safe space for people to share their deepest joys and their deepest pains.

READING

"Self-disclosure usually draws us closer to those who listen. To my mind this is the greatest effect of transparency. There's no guarantee that it will work that way every time. People can get turned off when they hear too much, too fast, from too many. But there's no question that a certain amount of openness is a necessary precondition for interpersonal intimacy. Breadth and depth of self-revelation is still the most reliable indication of the level of friendship. This relational fact of life has some tragic implications for those who have unfulfilled needs for affiliation. Loners are hesitant to take off their masks for fear of rejection. This very act of concealment, however, is destined to block the closeness they desperately desire."

Em Griffin, *Getting Together* (Downers Grove, IL: InterVarsity Press, 1982), 116.

RECOMMENDATIONS

1 The group must be told that honest sharing and loving listening is integral to the life of the group. This also means that the group must promise to keep confidential what is shared in the group and to obtain permission if they want to share what they heard in the group to those outside the group.

2 The group leader and the more mature members of the group must lead by example. They must demonstrate openness and honesty in their sharing.

3 Subdividing the group by gender and/or into smaller groups will help people to open up. Most people are hesitant to share in a large, mixed group. This is especially true if the group includes husbands and wives.

4

The risen Christ wants to **carry our burdens** and encourages us to **carry each other's burdens**

REFLECTION

"... but we had hoped that he was the one who was going to redeem Israel."
(LUKE 24:21a)

A healthy small group is also one where her members can find real help in times of need. We see the two disciples on the Emmaus road modelling for us this discipline of mutual burden bearing. They were both going through a very tough time in their lives. They had decided that Jesus was the promised Messiah that the prophets had said would come to deliver Israel. And now to their horror, Jesus had been captured, tortured, executed, and buried. Their hopes had been crushed. But they had each other. They did not bear their crushed hopes alone. They would eventually discover that in walking together, they would encounter the Christ who walked with them. When we walk with each other we experience the presence of the risen Christ.

Jesus said that in this world we would have troubles (John 16:33). Christian and non-Christian alike live in a fallen world with all its pain and brokenness. The final healing of this broken world awaits the coming of the new heavens and the new earth (Revelation 21:1–4). In the meantime, followers of Jesus are asked to take their burdens to Jesus because He cares for us (1 Peter 5:7). A healthy small group is a place where people encounter the real presence of Christ and therefore it should be a place where people can bring their burdens. A key way that Jesus reaches out to us is through another brother or sister in Christ, hence the call to bear one another's burdens. (Galatians 6:2)

A healthy small group, then, is not just an activity or a programme. It is a relationship. A small group is a place where a group of Christians live out Jesus's command "to love one another as He has loved us." (John 13:34)

Two things need to happen for a small group to be the caring community that it should be. First, as we have seen, there needs to be a commitment to transparent sharing. Next, the group must intentionally live out Paul's command to accept one another as Christ has accepted us (Romans 15:7). When a group extends the loving acceptance of Christ, group members will find the group a safe place to share their struggles.

This then is the fourth mark of a healthy small group. It is a caring community where her members carry each other's burdens as Christ carries their burdens.

READING

“‘Loving one another’ is the essential reality of life together in the ecclesia. In the small group, people should be more important than work. In the small group, being and relating are more important than doing. In the loving Christian community, being and relating define and direct the important work to be done. The love of persons is carried out through ‘actions’ that prove their verbal commitment to be the ‘truth’. The truth is love in action. As John’s epistle says, ‘This is how we know what love is: Jesus Christ laid down his life for us.’ In response and reciprocity the members of the ecclesia are called to lay down their lives for one another. The practice of love is the intentional and sacrificial sharing of persons and possessions with other members of the group.”

Gareth Weldon Icenogle, *Biblical Foundations For Small Group Ministry* (Downers Grove, IL: InterVarsity Press, 1994), 303.

Recommendations

1   Group members can begin to learn to share their lives with a simple exercise that can be done at the beginning of each meeting — every member shares one joy and one struggle he or she has experienced since the last time the group met.

2   To bear each other's burdens, group members will be encouraged to connect with one another outside official meeting times. In other words, the members of the group are to be committed to each other and not just to an activity, the regular group meeting.

3   Some burdens may need resources from outside the group. Group members can share their knowledge of possible sources of help.

5

The risen Christ invites others to Himself through us

REFLECTION

"But they urged him strongly, 'Stay with us, for it is nearly evening; the day is almost over.' So he went in to stay with them."
(LUKE 24:29)

One of the key marks of a healthy group is how they treat visitors and guests. When a group has been meeting for some time it tends to look inwards and subconsciously or consciously becomes exclusive. First-time visitors to the group feel excluded. They may not return. What is worse, they do not experience the welcoming love of God. For our God is:

> ... a refuge for the poor,
> a refuge for the needy in their
> distress,
> a shelter from the storm
> and a shade from the heat.
> (Isaiah 25:4a)

A healthy group understands that the risen Christ is in their midst and that He reaches out through them.

The writer of Hebrews reminds us, "Do not forget to show hospitality to strangers, for by so doing some people have shown hospitality to angels without knowing it." (Hebrews 13:2)

The two disciples on the Emmaus road demonstrated this practice when they invited Jesus to join them for their evening meal and to stay the night in the warmth and security of their home.

Luke reminds us that the early church:

> ...broke bread in their homes and ate together with glad and sincere hearts, praising God and enjoying the favor of all the people. And the Lord added to their number daily those who were being saved. (Acts 2:46b–47)

If the church had new members daily, they *had* to be a welcoming community.

Followers of Jesus are called to love God and neighbour (Luke 10:25–28). A key way we show our love for God is to love people. This includes the commitment of group members to bear each other's burdens and the commitment to bless all whom God brings to the group. Love is not a strategy to grow the group or to grow the church. It is an expression of God's love through us, and people will know the difference.

This then is the fifth mark of a healthy group — visitors are warmly welcomed.

READING

"Providing hospitality and welcome to friends and strangers is consistently highlighted in Scripture as a Christian practice.... We seem to have a choice: either we can avoid the intimacy of fully welcoming 'the other' or we can lean into it, knowing that extending this kind of welcome is another step toward fostering the transforming community we seek. In fact, the choice to open our homes to one another is so countercultural today that it might be as significant as choosing what book or Bible study we will engage together! After all, it was during an ordinary, spur-of-the-moment meal in someone's ordinary home that the disciples' eyes were opened and they recognized the fact that this 'stranger' was no stranger at all!"

Ruth Haley Barton, *Life Together In Christ* (Downers Grove, IL: InterVarsity Press, 2014), 44–45.

RECOMMENDATIONS

1   The leaders and members of the group must state upfront and often that loving visitors and making them feel welcome is a key part of the life of the group. In any review of the life of the group, the group must be honest to check how they are doing in this aspect of group life.

2   Assign someone to help introduce a visitor to the members of the group and to the activities of the group. This may be the member who invited the newcomer or someone else designated for the purpose. He or she should sit with the guest, helping him or her understand the activities of the group, e.g. why we sing, what we are hoping to get out of the Bible study, etc.

3   Invite the newcomer to contribute to the life of the group in ways that are comfortable for them. For example, they could contribute food in one of the group's meals. Participation helps integration.

6

The risen Christ
calls us to **witness**
for Him in the world

REFLECTION

"They got up and returned at once to Jerusalem. There they found the eleven and those with them, assembled together."
(LUKE 24:33)

Another key trait of a healthy group is that they share Christ with those outside their group. Therefore, groups that are inward looking and exist only for the needs of those in the group, are not healthy. Any genuine encounter with the risen Christ must lead to a desire to share Him with others.

The first thing the two disciples did when they realised that they had been with Christ and that He had risen from the dead was to rush back to share the good news with their friends. This meant a seven-mile walk in the dark. But when you have encountered the living Christ, and you realise that He is indeed the Messiah and that indeed the Kingdom of God has arrived in Him, you can't help but want to share the good news with others.

Later in Luke's gospel, Jesus Himself tells us that we need to witness to Him.

> He told them, "This is what is written: The Messiah will suffer and rise from the dead on the third day, and

repentance for the forgiveness of sins will be preached in his name to all nations, beginning at Jerusalem. You are witnesses of these things. I am going to send you what my Father has promised; but stay in the city until you have been clothed with power from on high." (Luke 24:46–49)

How do we share Christ? We take our cues from Jesus. He witnessed to the good news of the Kingdom through word and deed, through proclamation and demonstration. He preached the good news, calling people to repent, that is, to reorientate their lives by returning to the loving Kingship of God. He also witnessed to the good news through deeds — He would minister to those with desperate need, e.g. the sick, the hungry, the demonised, etc., (Matthew 4:23–25) to show that the Kingdom of God had drawn near.

A healthy group witnesses for Christ by sharing the gospel of Christ to those who do not know Him and by touching lives with the love of Christ. We can only do it in the power of the Spirit but we must do it.

This then is the sixth mark of a healthy group — it witnesses to the risen Christ in the power of His Spirit.

READING

"Mission is sharing in word and deed the good news of Christ's love to people in need. Christians, individually and together, must reach beyond themselves. As God's 'divine power has granted to us all things that pertain to life and godliness' (2 Pet 1:3), we are responsible to apply his power and love to change individuals and society....

Mission encompasses the broadest concept of sharing God's love in word and deed. It's more than simply supplying food to the hungry. It's more than simply proclaiming the human need to repent and believe. Outreach includes evangelism *and* social action....

The biblical mandate includes both doing 'the work of an evangelist' (1 Tim 4:5) and loving 'in deed and in truth' (1 Jn 3:18)."

Steve Barker et al., *Good Things Come In Small Groups* (Downers Grove, IL: InterVarsity Press, 1985), 111–112.

RECOMMENDATIONS

1   The group must be told upfront and reminded regularly that the group exists not just for the members but that the group also exists to witness for Christ to a fallen world.

2   The group should always be praying and thinking about how they can share the gospel with those who do not know Christ. They could maintain a list of people they hope to see come to follow Christ that the group prays for on a regular basis. The group could link up with church outreach initiatives like Alpha.

3   The group should be thinking and praying about how they can witness to the gospel through deeds. Either as a group or working in conjunction with churches and para-church groups, they can help to meet human needs in Jesus's name and help the members think through how to demonstrate God's values in their work and in other facets of their life.

4   Ministry must be an outflow of a real relationship with Christ. Therefore the group's walk with the risen Christ must be kept fresh. The group must set apart time to pray for the Lord to guide and empower the group as they seek to witness for Christ.

7

The risen Christ **meets** with us over meals

REFLECTION

"When he was at the table with them, he took bread, gave thanks, broke it and began to give it to them. Then their eyes were opened and they recognized him, and he disappeared from their sight."
(LUKE 24:30–31)

It is hard to talk about eating in a world troubled by both gluttony and starvation. But we all need to eat to live. It is in many ways the most human of all our activities. When we eat together with others, we relax, we slow down, and enter into conversations that allow the sharing of our lives. The last mark of a healthy small group is that they eat together regularly and share their lives as they share their meals.

We note that the two disciples recognised Jesus when they were seated for a meal. Revelation came over the bread and wine and the other dishes on the table. Some see in this a symbol of the Lord's Supper/Holy Communion. While this may be true, what is happening here in Luke 24 is a regular evening meal, not a symbolic one. Meals are very important in the Bible because meals both symbolise and strengthen relationships. An invitation to a meal was an invitation to a relationship, and regular shared meals helped to strengthen relationships. Indeed, sharing meals together in homes was a regular practice of the early church (Acts 2:42–47). It should be a practice of a healthy small group.

Eating together is also important because it helps to strengthen the other components of healthy small-group life. Over meals, we:

- recognise the presence of the living Christ;

- encounter Christ as we share what He says to us in the Word;

- have conversations that allow us to be transparent and to share our stories;

- share our struggles that we may receive support and help;

- invite friends, including those who may need to join a group or those who need to know the living Christ; and

- "spur one another on to love and good deeds" (Hebrews 10:24).

I know many groups have refreshments after the meeting and that is very helpful. Indeed, often, it is in the informal conversations over refreshments that significant ministry takes place. But the benefits of sharing life over meals happens better over a main meal like lunch or dinner.

This then is the seventh mark of a healthy group — they share meals together.

READING

"One of the most powerful expressions of mutuality and friendship is sharing a meal together. We tend to eat with people we like and with people who are like us. But shared meals break down social boundaries. All of us need to eat, and when we break bread together we embody our solidarity and common humanity.

Meals are also at the heart of the Christian story. Jesus frequently ate with his followers, adversaries and outcasts in the community. He was sometimes a guest and sometimes a host, but in either case, meals were important settings where he shared deep truths and insights about the kingdom, discipleship and God's priorities.... An important spiritual discipline around meals is to ask ourselves regularly, *With whom am I eating? Who is invited, and who is left out?* Our meals become kingdom meals especially when people who are usually overlooked find a place — a place of welcome and value."

Christopher L. Heuertz & Christine D. Pohl, *Friendship at the Margins* (Downers Grove, IL: InterVarsity Press, 2010), 80–81.

RECOMMENDATIONS

1   Where possible, start a meeting with a main meal, like lunch or dinner. If the meeting is held on a weeknight, it may have to start a little later to give members time to travel to the meeting from work.

2   If the host needs help with providing food, members can help contribute dishes to the meal or contribute financially so that the host and/or other group members can buy cooked food for the meal. Group members should also help lay the table and clean up after the meeting.

3   In some sense, all meals are sacramental and in thanking God for the food we remember Christ and His provision of life. If your church tradition allows, the group could also incorporate the Lord's Supper into the meal.

Conclusion

As in many things in the Christian faith, renewal comes not from following some technique, but from drawing closer to our Lord. If we want to see our church small groups thriving we need to return to the recognition of the presence of the living Christ in our midst. We have looked at seven marks of a healthy small group. We will restate them here.

Healthy small groups have members who:

1 gather around the presence of the risen Christ;

2 listen to the risen Christ speaking to them through the study of the Word;

3 imitate the risen Christ by speaking the truth in love to each other;

4 bear each other's burdens as representatives of the risen Christ who bears their burdens;

5 allow the risen Christ to extend His welcome through them;

6 share the risen Christ with others; and

7 celebrate the presence of the risen Christ over shared meals.

The first six marks attend to the three key relationships of every disciple — with the Lord, with other disciples and with the world that needs the gospel.

RELATING WITH THE LORD

1   Gather around the presence of Christ.

2   Listen to Christ speak to them through the study of the Word.

RELATING WITH EACH OTHER

3   Imitate Christ by speaking the truth in love to each other.

4   Bear each other's burdens as representatives of a Christ who bears their burdens.

RELATING TO A LOST WORLD

5   Allow Christ to extend His welcome through them.

6   Share Christ with others.

THE LAST MARK IS A CELEBRATION OF THE PRESENCE OF CHRIST THAT HELPS EMPOWER THE OTHER SIX MARKS.

7 Celebrate the presence of Christ over shared meals.

When a group takes seriously the seven marks of a healthy group they are in fact nurturing the three major relationships of every Christian — with God, with each other, and with a world that needs Christ.

The need for the gospel has never been greater. All followers of Jesus need to be all they are meant to be in Christ so that they can shine for Christ. Christians grow best when they are part of healthy small groups. And healthy small groups are Christ-centred ones.

ABOUT THE AUTHOR

Since 1985, Soo Inn has been journeying with
people through his ministry of preaching/
teaching, writing, and mentoring. Originally
trained as a dentist at the University of
Singapore, he answered God's call to go into
full-time church-related ministry in 1981 and
obtained his Master of Theology from Regent
College, Vancouver, Canada, in 1984. In 2006,
he obtained his Doctor of Ministry from Fuller
Theological Seminary, California.

His primary passions include connecting the
Word of God to the struggles of daily life, and
the promotion of the discipline of spiritual
friendship. He has been a supporter of Arsenal
Football Club since 1971 and his favourite
movie is Star Wars 4.